The Empty Suit of Armour

D1079780

Also by Kaye Umansky and Keren Ludlow

The Night I Was Chased by a Vampire
The Spooks Step Out
The Bogey Men and the Trolls Next Door

The Empty Suit of Armour

KAYE UMANSKY

Illustrated by Keren Ludlow

A Dolphin
Paperback

Published in paperback in 1996

This edition published in 1999

First published in Great Britain in 1995
by Orion Children's Books
a division of the Orion Publishing Group Ltd
Orion House
5 Upper St Martin's Lane
London WC2H 9EA

A CIP catalogue record for this book is available
from the British Library

Printed in Great Britain by Clays Ltd, St Ives plc

ISBN 1 85881 251 8

In a castle on a hillside
On a cold and moonlit night

The mice behind the wainscot
Got a very nasty fright . . .

And an owl up in the rafters
Gave a sudden, startled hoot
As an Empty Suit of Armour
Raised its arm in a salute.

Its helmet swivelled slowly
With a harsh, metallic squeal.
It tested out its knee joints
Just to see how they would feel . . .

Then it brushed away a cobweb
And it stood up really straight,
And clanked across the hallway
With a strangely jerky gait.

The castle doors swung open
(In the creaky way they do)
And the Empty Suit of Armour
Very squeakily marched through.

The night was cold and frosty
But it didn't seem to care.
It stomped across the courtyard
With a most determined air.

It didn't stop to grab a hat,
Or bother with a coat.
The drawbridge slowly lowered
And it marched across the moat.

It set off down the hillside
(Which was really rather steep)
Giving headaches to the hedgehogs
And deafening the sheep.

A poor old shabby shepherd
Sipping soup upon a rock
Spilled the contents of his thermos
Down his shabby shepherd's smock –

SCREAM

Dropped his crook into a crevice
And his sandwich in a stream –
Then bolted like a rabbit,
With a startled little scream.

SPLOSH!

At the bottom lay a forest
Just as dark as dark can be
With a hundred hungry predators
Behind each bush and tree.

There were wolves and wily weasels,
There were vipers, there were voles,
There were ferrets, there were foxes,
There were things that lurked in holes . . .

But the Armour marched on by them,
Making such a fearful racket
That no one liked to be the first
To jump out and attack it.

At the far end of the forest
Was a quiet country lane
Which led to a wee village
(Little Romping-In-The-Rain).

Just a quiet little village,
With a peaceful little brook,
The sort of place where folks
Retire early, with a book.

LITTLE ROMPING
IN-THE-RAIN

Up the lane the Armour clattered
With a bold, defiant rattle,
Past a torn and tatty scarecrow
And some very puzzled cattle.

29

A farmer sipping cider
In the local village inn
Turned his head towards the window
At the fast approaching din.

Then the farmer spied the Armour –
And his eyes grew ever wider,
His face went pale and with a wail
He fainted in his cider!

The lights came on in cottages
And people stared in fright
At the Empty Suit of Armour
Who had spoiled their early night.

A dog came up to sniff it
With its ears laid low and flat.
Then it backed away stiff-legged.
No. It wouldn't mess with that.

The Armour kept on going,
Past the churchyard and the mill,
And it left that little village
And marched onwards, up the hill.

All that night it kept on going
With a stiff, relentless tread
Till the sun filled the horizon
And the moon went home to bed.

Now the road became a thoroughfare,
A place of squealing brakes
Of motor cars and lorries
Bearing Mr Creemy's cakes . . .

WHOOSH!

Of juggernauts and caravans
And motorbikes and scooters
And little grey-haired grannies
Honking madly on their hooters.

But the Empty Suit of Armour
Simply plunged into the fray
And marched right down the middle,
Just assuming right of way.

The road led to a market town
That buzzed with cheerful chatter
As the early morning shoppers
Stood about and had a natter.

But there fell a heavy silence
At the shrill cry of dismay . . .
"There's an Empty Suit of Armour
And its heading right this way!"

The crowds fell back respectfully
To let the Armour through,
Alarmed, but rather curious
To see what it would do.

And this is what the Armour did.
It reached a sudden stop.
It turned around quite slowly
Then it went into a shop . . .

And there it bought an oil can
And proceeded to anoint
Every nut and bolt and rivet,
Every shrilly shrieking joint.

And when at last the job was done,
It set the oil can down
And smoothly – slickly – silently –
It marched right out of town . . .

GLIDE SWISH

Back to the ruined castle
On that high and hilly ground,
Where it glided through the open doors
Without a single sound.

Then it took up its position
With its back against the wall.
Just an Empty Suit of Armour
In a dark, deserted hall.

So if you're ever walking
On a cold and moonlit night
And you hear the sound of marching –
Do not run away in fright.

SQUEAL
SQUEAK
CLATTER
RATTLE

Just nod and smile quite pleasantly
And show no consternation . . .
For it's just a Suit of Armour
On a quest for lubrication.